# Eight Dolphins of Katrina

This book is about people who have devoted their lives to saving dolphins. Their work benefits all of us. But we must never forget the residents of the Gulf Coast who endured so much, and the selfless people who stepped forward to help.

*To those who respect and care about the extraordinary creatures in the sea, including Billy, Brooke, Will, and Heather, and to Anna Webman, who made it happen.* — J.W.C.

*To the victims of Katrina.* — Y.N.

For information about permission to reproduce selections from this book, write to trade.permissions@hmhco.com or to Permissions, Houghton Mifflin Harcourt Publishing Company, 3 Park Avenue, 19th Floor, New York, New York 10016.

www.hmhco.com

The text of this book is set in Times.
The illustrations are watercolor, reproduced in full color.
Library of Congress Cataloging-in-Publication Data is on file.

ISBN: 978-0-547-71923-8 hardcover
ISBN: 978-0-544-93261-6 paperback

Manufactured in China
SCP 10 9 8 7 6 5 4 3
4500730238

# Eight Dolphins of Katrina

*A True Tale of Survival*

Written by Janet Wyman Coleman · Illustrated by Yan Nascimbene

Houghton Mifflin Harcourt · Boston   New York

The windows at the Marine Life Oceanarium in Gulfport, Mississippi, should have been black. Instead, the buildings glowed.

TIM HOFFLAND RAN ACROSS THE LAWN. He noticed a barrel wobbling in the wind. It fell over and spat trash into the air. The dolphin trainer watched dozens of paper cups and plates somersault into the bushes.

It was before dawn on August 28, 2005. The windows at the Marine Life Oceanarium in Gulfport, Mississippi, should have been black. Instead, the buildings glowed. The people on the Gulf Coast were wide awake.

"Hey, Tim," whispered Moby Solangi, the head of the Oceanarium. The trainer nodded and pulled the door shut behind him. Shannon Huyser and Marci Romagnoli, two other trainers, stared at weather reports on a computer.

"We don't have much time," Dr. Solangi told his trainers. "I've talked to the owners of two motels. They agreed to let us put our dolphins in their swimming pools. We'll transport three dolphins to the Best Western and three to the Holiday Inn. The motels are four miles inland, so the dolphins should be safe there. After that, you have to leave. Grab what you need and get out of here."

"What about the rest of the dolphins?" Tim asked. He wanted to say, *You can't leave Jackie behind!* She was an old dolphin and his favorite, but everyone had favorites.

"We don't have time to move all of them," Dr. Solangi replied. "The rest will stay in the large pool. It survived Hurricane Camille, and that was one of the biggest hurricanes on record. Besides, it's better not to have all the dolphins in one place."

Jackie circled the pool. Elijah followed closer than a shadow. Shelley skimmed the surface, leaving a trail of bubbles. Tamra rose out of the water as if pulled up by strings, and flipped. Kelly made a creaking sound like an old door, and disappeared beneath a splash. Noah swam backwards with a ball in his mouth.

Katelyn was the first on the canvas sling. She squirmed when it lifted her into the air. Water poured back into the pool. Cayenne was next, then Tessie. Three more dolphins were scooped up and taken away. Jackie, Toni, Shelley, Elijah, Kelly, Tamra, Noah, and Jill paid no attention.

Inside the trucks, Marci and Shannon sprayed the dolphins with cold water. Tim squeezed a sponge over Cayenne.

"You're going to be okay, Cayenne," he said softly. *I hope Jackie's going to be okay too,* he thought.

Two hours later, Brewer, Tessie, and Cherie were lowered into the Holiday Inn swimming pool. Katelyn, Jonah, and Cayenne slid into the pool at the Best Western. A few people stood in the rain and stared at the new guests.

Tim drove home. He stuffed a duffle bag with clothes and photos. Then he grabbed his guitars and his computer, and took a piece of cold pizza and a bottle of water from the refrigerator. With his favorite pillow under his arm, he shut the door and left.

Jackie circled the pool. Elijah followed closer than a shadow.

In the early morning hours of August 29, 2005, Hurricane Katrina slammed into the coasts of Mississippi and Louisiana. Huge trees swayed and crashed to the ground. Roofs and outdoor furniture twirled through the air like Frisbees. Water rose quickly, swamping streets, cars, and basements. The storm surge knocked down doors, sloshed across floors, and rose up staircases. Telephone and electric lines flew off their poles and snarled.

A forty-foot tidal wave washed over the Marine Life Oceanarium. It crushed the dolphin house. The metal rafters and roof plunged into the pool.

In the early morning hours of August 29, 2005, Hurricane Katrina slammed into the coasts of Mississippi and Louisiana.

The next day was sunny and quiet. Along the Gulf Coast, many of the buildings were gone.

The next day was sunny and quiet. Along the Gulf Coast, many of the buildings were gone. The ones that survived were badly damaged and surrounded by branches and trash. Roads were blocked by downed trees, flooded cars, walls from buildings, and crumbled chimneys.

Tim and Dr. Solangi made their way to the dolphin pool. *Please be okay, Jackie*, Tim thought as he avoided the power lines and garbage.

The pool was empty except for the mangled rafters and chunks of roof. Tim and Dr. Solangi stared at the small puddles on the bottom. Then they gazed at the peaceful waters of the Gulf of Mexico.

"Maybe the dolphins survived," Dr. Solangi said.

Tim thought, *How could they live through a roof falling onto their heads—or the force of a forty-foot tidal wave?*

"They could be out there," Dr. Solangi continued, "waiting for us. Tim, how much time do we have?"

"What do you mean?" Tim asked.

"We have to assume they've forgotten how to feed themselves," Dr. Solangi said. "They're so used to being fed by us. How long can they survive without food?"

"They're free to swim anywhere," Tim pointed out.

"The dolphins won't leave. They're connected to all of you, and the Oceanarium is their real home. How much time?"

"They have about a week. Maybe a little longer, unless they're injured. Then they won't last long."

Dr. Solangi started telephoning. He called anyone who might have a boat or a helicopter.

"Dolphins?" said a voice on the phone. "You want to rescue dolphins in the gulf? That's ridiculous!"

Dr. Solangi and the trainers had mourned the loss of a sick dolphin before, but never so many at once. Eight lives. Eight members of their extended family. They kept telephoning.

"You want a boat for what?" said another voice. "You're crazy! Those dolphins are long gone. And they're just dolphins."

Dr. Solangi and the trainers had mourned the loss of a sick dolphin before, but never so many at once. Eight lives.

Twelve days after Katrina roared through the Oceanarium, Dr. Solangi had a motorboat and a helicopter.

Twelve days after Katrina roared through the Oceanarium, Dr. Solangi had a motorboat and a helicopter.

"I guess we all believe in miracles," said Tim as he climbed into the boat, "or we wouldn't be here."

Dr. Solangi tightened his seatbelt in the helicopter and looked out at the horizon. Hurricane Rita was picking up strength and moving toward the coast. The helicopter rose up like a dragonfly.

"Cut the engines," Tim yelled from the bow of the boat. He picked up metal buckets and swung them together like cymbals. Marci and Shannon blew whistles and banged buckets too. *Where are you, Jackie?* Tim thought.

Overhead, the helicopter circled. Dr. Solangi scanned the surface of the water through binoculars. *We'll never find all eight of them,* he thought. *Maybe one or two.*

The crashing, whistling, and banging went on for fifteen minutes. Tim looked across miles of empty water and felt a wave of sadness. He imagined Jackie's eyes and her smile.

There was a soft clicking, but no one heard it. A dolphin swam under the boat.

"Tamra!" Shannon yelled. "Tamra?"

The buckets banged, the trainers shouted, and the helicopter whopped overhead.

An eighth dolphin surfaced.

A dolphin head popped out of the water. It was covered with scratches.

"Elijah!" Tim gasped. A second head appeared. Marci pointed and almost fell out of the boat.

"It's Noah!"

"There's Kelly!"

"Look! Toni!"

"There's Shelley!"

"Jill! Everyone, it's Jill!"

"Tamra! Oh, Tamra!"

Tim Hoffland couldn't breathe. He counted the dolphins, "One, two, three, four, five, six, seven."

Someone asked, "Where's Jackie?" Tim felt the other trainers turn toward him. He cleared his throat. *Poor Jackie,* he thought. *She was just too old.* His eyes filled with tears. Everyone looked away.

An eighth dolphin surfaced.

"Jackie," Tim whispered. He jumped into the water to be closer to his old friend. Jackie swam straight to Tim. She nuzzled his chest and squeaked with joy.

*How do we capture eight dolphins swimming in open water?*

The trainers threw fish filled with vitamins and medicines into the dolphins' large mouths. Then they took blood samples from the large tails to test for infections. The water in the gulf was polluted from the storm, so Dr. Solangi was determined to get the dolphins into tanks as soon as possible. He wondered, *How do we capture eight dolphins swimming in open water?*

An orange buoy from the Oceanarium was placed in the water. The dolphins discovered that if they returned to it, they would be fed. Meanwhile, Dr. Solangi and the trainers rushed to come up with a plan.

The trainers found a floating platform made of rubber mats. They put it in the water and taught the dolphins how to beach themselves on the seesawing surface. Five days after she was first sighted, Jackie slid up next to Tim. One by one, the dolphins were hoisted off the platform and lowered onto a boat. A television cameraman recorded the event.

"Finally, some good news for all you viewers!" said the commentator on the *Mississippi Nightly News.*

The story of the Katrina dolphins spread around the world. The dolphins survived, the experts said, because they stayed together and took care of each other. Instead of swimming away, they waited for their trainers to take them home.

The eight dolphins were transported to a tank at the U.S. Navy base in Gulfport, Mississippi. The six motel visitors joined them there.

At the base, Tim watched Jackie circle her tank. *She's safe,* he thought. *She's going to be okay.*

"We can go home now," he said to Marci and Shannon. No one answered.

"Maybe we should celebrate?" Tim suggested. *I'm so tired,* he thought. *I'm not sure my legs will move.* He noticed that the other trainers looked exhausted too.

"You know," Tim said, "it's not easy being in a strange new home. Maybe the dolphins need company."

The trainers found cots and placed them near the tank.

Then they lay down and went right to sleep.

The eight dolphins were transported to a tank at the U.S. Navy base in Gulfport, Mississippi.

# More About Man's Best Friend

Millions of years ago, dolphins strolled around on land. If you look at a dolphin's skeleton, you will discover the remnants of legs. Scientists think that they resembled wolves but they probably behaved like cows. When food became scarce, dolphins waded into the water to look for more.

Thousands of years ago, the Greeks believed that dolphins carried messages from the god of the sea, Poseidon. In one Greek myth, Poseidon changed sailors into dolphins and made them rescuers. In *Eight Dolphins of Katrina,* people saved dolphins. In other true stories, the dolphin is the hero.

One hundred years ago, Mark Twain yelled, "Here comes Pelorus Jack!" The American writer had traveled to New Zealand to see a world celebrity. A photo of the dolphin had even been on the cover of the *Illustrated London News*! For twenty-four years, from 1888 through 1912, Pelorus Jack met ships in Pelorus Sound and, riding the bow wave, steered them through the rocks of French Pass. In 1904, a passenger on the deck of the *Penguin* fired a shot at the famous guide. New Zealanders quickly passed a law forbidding anyone from harming him. Sadly, Pelorus Jack avoided the *Penguin*. Five years later, the ship hit the rocks and sank.

In 2000, a dolphin off the coast of southeastern Italy became separated from his pod. Fillipo (a name given to him by local residents) was so friendly that he became a tourist attraction. On August 8, Davide Ceci fell overboard near the town of Manfredonia. He was fourteen years old, and he couldn't swim. At first, the boy's father, who was still on the boat, didn't notice. As Davide sank, he felt something pushing him up from below. He realized it was Fillipo, so he held on. The dolphin zeroed in on the boat and swam alongside. The astonished father leaned over and grabbed his son.

Dolphins have also rescued dogs and much larger wild animals. On March 10, 2008, a female pygmy sperm whale and her calf became stranded on Mahia Beach in New Zealand. For an hour and a half, members of the Department of Conservation tried to guide the whales back to deeper waters. They were about to give up when a large, chirping dolphin arrived. The two whales relaxed, and then followed the dolphin out to sea.

Who are these animal rescuers? Scientists have told us that dolphins have a very large brain for their body size, just like humans. They have their own language, and they love to play games. Dolphins have been spotted in the ocean tossing clumps of seaweed back and forth. Sometimes, they sneak up behind a pelican and pluck a tailfeather, or roll a sea turtle. Dolphins are cherished in many parts of the world, but in a few places (such as Japan and the Faroe Islands), they're slaughtered for food or celebration. People, boats, sharks, and pollution are their biggest enemies.

They say that a dog is man's best friend, but that's on land. In the water, it will always be the dolphin.

# An *Eight Dolphins* Scrapbook

This is the Marine Life Oceanarium before August 29, 2005.

Jackie performs a ring jump for Marci before Hurricane Katrina.

Eli and Noah gliding and posing before the hurricane.

On August 28, 2005, six dolphins were moved to motel swimming pools. Tim Hoffland is in the pool on the right with his arms around Kelly. Dr. Solangi is in the middle of the photo in the back.

On August 29, 2005, Hurricane Katrina battered the Gulf coast. It was the worst natural disaster in the history of the United States. The Marine Life Oceanarium was completely destroyed.

This photo from September 2, 2005, shows the dolphin tank after it had been crushed by a forty-foot wave.

On September 10, 2005, the search for the eight dolphins began.

The rescue boat drifted in open water.

Fifteen minutes after the rescuers started blowing their whistles, all eight dolphins surfaced near the boat.

The dolphins had been taught to present their tails in order to have their blood drawn for medical tests.

"The dolphins went through so much," said a trainer, "but they still trusted us."

Here, Tim and Marci teach Jackie how to beach herself on the mat. On September 15, Jackie was lifted off the mats and lowered onto a boat.

The trainers watch Kelly, Shelley, and Elijah taking a bow in the Gulf of Mexico.

Other organizations contributed to the rescue, including the National Oceanic and Atmospheric Administration (NOAA), Harbor Branch Oceanographic Institute, the U.S. Navy, Gulfarium and Gulf World (two oceanariums), and the U.S. Coast Guard.

One by one, the dolphins were transported back to the harbor. They were taken to the U.S. Navy base in Gulfport, Mississippi.

On September 20, twenty-two days after Katrina, the last four dolphins joined the others in the saltwater tank.

Tim places a tube down Tessie's throat in order to hydrate her. Dolphins get most of their water from food. Like humans, they can't drink salty ocean water.

If you look closely, you can see the scratches on Toni and Tamra.

# Notes on the Eight Dolphins of Katrina

**Elijah,** the youngest dolphin at four years old, is very brave. When he was found, he had a stinger embedded in his forehead. The trainers think he was curious about a stingray and got a little too close.

**Noah,** Kelly's son, is a troublemaker. He likes to nip the trainers' feet when they're in the pool. Is he wondering, *Where are their fins?* The flukes (tail) and dorsal fin of a dolphin are made of cartilage, like a human nose.

**Toni** is funny and noisy. Underwater, dolphins emit sound waves from their foreheads. When the waves hit a fish or other object, they bounce back like an echo. This process, which is called echolocation, allows the dolphins to "hear" an object's size, location, and speed.

**Shelley** is stubborn. She doesn't like having her blood drawn during her regular checkups. Who does? Veterinarians check the dolphins' blood once a month to make sure the animal is healthy.

**Tamra** is a very sweet dolphin. At one point, she had cancer. Dolphins get pneumonia, stomach ulcers, rashes, infected cuts, and scrapes just like humans.

**Jackie** loves to work and play with the trainers in the water. She is happy to jump, flip, spin, bow, and tail walk. Many dolphins make forty to fifty acrobatic leaps in a row!

**Kelly** has beautiful natural markings and an engaging personality. She always trusts the trainers to be gentle with her babies. Female dolphins can produce six to eight calves over a lifetime.

**Jill** is strong-willed and a real leader. At forty years old, she is the oldest of the eight dolphins. Sometimes her teeth get loose and fall out. Bottlenose dolphins have seventy-six to one hundred teeth, so they have a few to spare.

"It was never a job," said one trainer. "It was our world."

# Sources

On March 18, 2009, I interviewed Dr. Delphine Vanderpool Shannon, Dr. Moby A. Solangi, and the three dolphin trainers—Tim, Marci, and Shannon—at the Institute for Marine Mammal Studies in Gulfport, Mississippi. Most of the information in this book came from those interviews and from follow-up conversations with Dr. Shannon. I am so grateful to them for sharing their story. —J.W.C.

The following secondary sources inspired the stories in "More About Man's Best Friend":

European Cetacean Bycatch Campaign. "Dolphin Saves Boy's Life." August 30, 2000. www.eurocbc.org/page158.html

Hutching, Gerard. "Dolphins." *Te Ara—the Encyclopedia of New Zealand*. Updated September 24, 2011. www.TeAra.govt.nz/en/dolphins/5/2 .

Malvern, James. "How Moko the Dolphin Gave Humans a Masterclass in Saving Stranded Whales." *Times* (London), March 13, 2008. www.timesonline.co.uk/tol/news/environment/article3540973.ece.

All photographs were provided by The Institute for Marine Mammal Studies.

## The Institute for Marine Mammal Studies Mission Statement

The Institute for Marine Mammal Studies (IMMS) is a non profit organization established in 1984 for the purposes of public education, conservation, and research of marine mammals and turtles in the wild and under human care. IMMS promotes public awareness of marine conservation issues through its research as well as its involvement in the community, encouraging citizens to be good stewards of the environment. Together with its scientific collaborators, IMMS hopes to make a significant impact on the health and well-being of dolphins and sea turtles in the Mississippi Sound and adjacent waters of the Northern Gulf of Mexico.

# Acknowledgments

I thank the following people for their invaluable contributions to this book and to the lives of many dolphins and other sea animals: Dr. Delphine Vanderpool Shannon, Dr. Moby A. Solangi, Tim Hoffland, Marci Romagnolis, Shannon Huyser. Also, I wish to thank Christine Krones and Erica Zappy. —J.W.C.

The Institute for Marine Mammal Studies wishes to sincerely thank the following organizations and agencies who made significant donations and contributions toward the animal rescues in the aftermath of Hurricane Katrina: Gulf World Marine Park; Florida's Gulfarium; Sea World, Orlando, FL; Harbor Branch Oceanographic Institute; National Oceanic and Atmospheric Administration; United States Department of Agriculture; US Navy Marine Mammal Program; Naval Construction Battalion Center—Gulfport, MS; Holiday Inn—Gulfport, MS; Best Western Seaway Inn—Gulfport, MS; Memorial Hospital of Gulfport; US FoodService; the Mirage Resort and Casino, Las Vegas, NV; Harrison County Sheriff's Department; Hancock County Sheriff's Department; US Coast Guard; Florida Fish and Wildlife Conservation Commission; Friends of Animals of the Coastal Empire—Atlanta, GA; Mississippi Department of Marine Resources. Additionally, IMMS would like to thank the many other organizations and individuals that made generous donations.